How to Survive in Extreme Weather Conditions – Midwestern United States

These tips are adapted from various public access websites as well as my personal experience of living in a rural area of Ohio. I have survived bitterly cold winters (minus 18 degrees without counting wind chill), blizzards, 100 degree summers (without a/c), one tornado, floods, thunderstorms and other extreme conditions.

The first and most important tip: Be prepared. Have a fully charged cell phone nearby at all times. Smartphones are a great invention, but you might want to consider buying a cheaper phone, one that has few bells and whistles but also is not a memory hog, for emergency use as a back-up. Get one where you can buy minutes instead of having another monthly service charge.

Before we get started on how to survive specific extreme weather conditions, let's make a general list of essentials to keep on hand in the event we cannot get out and shop for a few days.

Stockpile your favorite foods and cut back or eliminate all together ones that are recommended but you don't like. It would be bad enough being stranded without having to eat things you don't like.

Most important is bottled water. Buy it by the gallon, because you are going to need it. A good estimate would be two gallons for each person, per day, up to a week. If you have pets, add a gallon per day. If you live in the country and use an electric pump, stash more water for sanitary purposes. This is one time hoarding is a good thing.

Build up a reserve by getting a few extra items during your weekly shopping trip and putting them away. Keep canned foods in a cool (34 to 70 degrees Fahrenheit) dry, dark place. Rotate your stock so that you will use the oldest first. Discard food with dents or broken seals.

- Bottled water.
- Canned goods. Fruit, tuna, chicken, vegetables, soup, juice.
- Mechanical can opener. To be safe, have two.
- Canned or powdered milk.
- Peanut butter.
- Jelly.
- Cereal.
- Crackers.
- Cookies.
- If caffeine is important to you (as it is to millions), tea, instant coffee, hot chocolate mix, Coca Cola or Pepsi.
- Chocolate candy.
- Food for people with special dietary needs, if applicable.
- Prescription meds, if applicable.
- Baby food and formula, if applicable.
- Dog and cat food, if applicable.
- Paper plates, plastic utensils.
- Plastic zippered kitchen bags.
- Plastic trash bags.
- Bath tissue (as my mother called toilet paper – it does sound more ladylike).
- Feminine hygiene needs, if applicable.
- Baby wipes.
- Hand sanitizer.
- Band-aids, aspirin, hydrogen peroxide.
- Flashlight for every room and new batteries.
- Battery operated radio with plenty of fresh batteries.

- Sleeping bag. If you have no heat and no way to get to a warm shelter, hunker down inside a sleeping bag. Cuddle with a loved one, if possible.
- Cash.
- Shovel.
- Duct tape.
- Books, magazines, scrapbooks – anything to help relax you while you wait for the danger to subside.
- At least one fully charged cell phone.

If you need to evacuate, make sure that your exit route will be clear. Driving on a road that is flooded, icy, with deep snow drifts, littered with debris (falling limbs), covered with downed power lines or congested with traffic is potentially deadly. Call for emergency services personnel if necessary.

Cold, Frigid, Weather.

The World Health Organization recommends keeping your thermostat 68 degrees for elderly, very young, or people with health problems. For healthy people, 64 degrees is the lowest recommended temperature. To save money and still be safe, 74 degrees is the upper limit.

During a blizzard when my mother's heating oil ran out she survived by hunkering down into a sleeping bag, putting a warm scarf over her head and face and sitting as close as safely possible to an electric heater until she could be rescued. With winds over 70 mph and visibility near zero, it was impossible for anyone to help her until after the storm was over.

Hyperthermia can occur even indoors. Confusion, memory loss, drowsiness, exhaustion, slurred speech and shivering are early warning signs. Infants may have cold, bright red skin and be lethargic.

Take serious precautions to reduce hyperthermia and frostbite when outdoors. Stay inside during frigid temperatures and windy conditions unless it is absolutely necessary to be outside.

According to the Mayo Clinic, frostbite occurs most commonly on fingers, toes, nose, ears, cheeks and chin. Due to skin numbness, you might not be aware that you have frostbite until someone else points it out.

The first sign of frostbite is cold skin and a prickly sensation. Numbness is the next step, followed by your skin turning red, white, bluish-white or grayish-yellow. Hard or waxy looking skin, stiff joints and muscles, and blistering after rewarming in severe cases are other symptoms.

If you are out in freezing cold without adequate gloves (as I have done on several occasions; there is no excuse for this behavior but I thought it would be safe to get to my car and warm it up) or your gloves get wet, get out of the weather if possible, then unzip or unbutton your coat just enough to allow you to put your bare hands under your armpits. Your inner thighs can also serve as an emergency hand warmer. This might sound ridiculous, but we are talking about surviving extreme weather.

Seek medical attention for frostbite if you experience white or pale skin, numbness, or blisters or fever.

Hyperthermia is a condition in which your body loses heat faster than it can be produced. Signs and symptoms of hypothermia include severe shivering, slurred speech, drowsiness and loss of coordination. Seek immediate medical attention if you experience these symptoms.

Cold weather puts extra stress on the heart, so if you have high blood pressure or any cardiac problems do not shovel snow or perform strenuous exercise outdoors. If you must go outside, dress appropriately, in several thin layers.

One of the best things about winter are the clothes. You choose functional outerwear or you can wear bright colors in flattering styles.

Down parkas are expensive but worth the cost. You can also wear a quilted or fake fur vest under a long waterproof coat.

Wear a hat. Although your head wear doesn't have to be stylish, it doesn't need to be boring, either, unless that is what you want. You can look cute especially with one of the plush or knit fleece lined animal hats, some of which come with built in ear flaps and mittens. A white wolf especially appeals to me.

Wear waterproof boots, lined if possible. You can also wear boots a size or two larger with thick socks. Although wool often is recommended, synthetic fuzzy socks are better for those of us who are allergic. You can also wear two pairs. My brother wears cotton next to his skin with wool over top. This combo keeps scratchy material away from his feet and ankles and the recommended wool as a barrier to ice and cold.

Boots should have soles and heels suitable for walking on ice and through slush. I had a pair of suede ankle high boots lined with synthetic fur. Oh, so warm! And with slick soles, oh, so dangerous! After falling a few times (some of us are oh, so stubborn), I realized they needed replaced and replaced they were.

Wear gloves! Any are better than nothing. I wear stretchy gloves under thicker, warmer ones. Knitted gloves with "touch" fingertips are available in every price range. Consider carrying hand warmers in your coat pockets, just in case.

You do have warm, cozy, soft sweaters, don't you? I buy them at end of season clearance sales each year. Scratchy, uncomfortable sweaters can be tolerated by wearing long sleeved cotton blouses underneath, but isn't winter bad enough without making yourself a long suffering martyr?

In bitter cold, wear long underwear or tights under pants. Snow pants are a better choice than jeans as wet jeans can contribute to frostbite. Wear wool slacks if you aren't allergic.

Keep dry.

If being stylish is not your first priority (and winter survival demands that function triumphs over fashion), check out military surplus websites for practical clothing at reasonable prices.

In an emergency, stuff your coat sleeves and pant legs with crumpled up newspaper. In years past, newspaper was commonly used to insulate houses and in some unfortunate cases as a substitute for blankets.

If your home is warm (or warm enough) and you don't absolutely need to go out in frigid or sub-zero weather, stay inside. Cuddle up beneath covers, by yourself or with a loved one (dogs are an excellent choice), and drink coffee, tea, heated and cinnamon spiced cider or hot chocolate – and let the world go on without you.

Keeping Your Home Warm – and Safe.

Natural gas, oil, kerosene, gasoline, wood and coal produce carbon monoxide, an odorless and colorless gas, which is deadly if burned without adequate ventilation. If you use a wood burner, you must have a clean (no creosote build up) working chimney attached to the stove. Oil, gas and coal furnaces must also been properly set up. Kerosene and gasoline are (in my opinion) too dangerous to even consider. Never use a barbecue grill indoors.

High levels of carbon monoxide can kill you, so please take great care in how you heat your house. If you are exposed to carbon monoxide, you might feel like you have the flu without a fever. Headaches, fatigue, dizziness, shortness of breath along with nausea and vomiting are possible early signs of carbon monoxide poisoning, followed by loss of consciousness, then death.

Electric space heaters must be used with caution. Make sure the heater turns itself off if it tips over and keep flammable materials at least three feet from heater. Discard heaters with frayed cords. I use them in the coldest of weather and replace them every few years. Some seasons they sell out before winter sets in and other years there are a few left over, sold on clearance.

Another cold weather worry is frozen water pipes. In bitter cold weather, I open my faucets to allow them to drip and sometimes even let them run a tiny but steady stream. Open cabinet doors to let warm air get to pipes. If possible, get pipes insulated and/or wrap with heat tape. Keep room temperature no lower than 55 degrees.

If your pipes do freeze, turn faucets on full blast. This alone will sometimes thaw pipes. However, you can't leave the house in case the water does come back on as you don't want a flood. Thaw pipes with a hair dryer. Never use a torch or other open flame as you could cause a fire. To avoid getting a (possibly fatal) shock, do not use your hair dryer or any other electric appliance in or near standing water.

If you live in an apartment building, contact the property manager. In many communities there are laws mandating that adequate temperatures must be maintained.

If you need help paying winter heating bills, investigate HEAP (Home Energy Assistance Program) in your area. Also see if your power company can put you on a budget and even out your payments throughout the year.

Local thrift stores and charities may be able to provide warm clothing, inexpensively. I shop winter clearance sales at local discount stores and stock up on new sweaters, jeans and coats for the next year.

If your power goes out, don't panic.   First, check your electric panel to make sure you haven't blown a circuit. This is a common occurrence when a person plugs in an additional space heater during cold weather.

If the fault is not in your house, call your utility company to report the outage. Keep their number in your phone and be patient as it is sometimes difficult to get through. When my power goes out instead of worrying about it, I pile on the covers and get some sleep.

Turn off the power strip to your computer and turn off your tv and all lights but one. Otherwise, there will be a power surge when the electricity is restored. The light that you left on will alert you when the power does come back on.

Stay in the house if at all possible. Do not go near downed power lines. If you must drive, be cautious. If the traffic lights are out, treat intersections as four way stops. Watch out for the other guy.

Stay warm. Wear a sweater or sweatshirt, jacket or coat, gloves and a winter hat. Cuddle up under a blanket if you are still cold.

Call elderly or disabled neighbors to make sure they are warm and safe. Don't hesitate to call emergency services so that they may be taken to a shelter.

Although many people have generators, I refused my son's kind offer to buy me one. I am not an electrician and I don't take unnecessary risks. If you are able to install and operate one safely, you are ahead of the game.

If you do buy a generator, take the time to learn everything you need to know.

To keep food fresh and at the proper temperature, keep your refrigerator and freezer doors closed.

Winter Safety Tips for Pets.

If there are outdoor cats in your neighborhood, bang on the hood and hook your horn before starting your car. Cats sometimes seek warmth on top of wheels or under the hood and can be killed by the fan belt of a car whose engine is running.

Also check your clothes dryer before turning it on as a cat might have sneaked in while you had the door open and were busy with the laundry.

Clean up any anti-freeze spills. I lost my beloved Harvey due to someone else's careless disposal of this necessary, but deadly, chemical treatment.

We all know not to leave our pets in cars during the summer, but it is also important that you not leave him there in winter, either. He could freeze to death.

If your dog is elderly, a puppy, ill, or otherwise sensitive to cold, let him out only to relieve himself. In bitter cold, I prefer cleaning up after my aged dog to risking his health or worrying about him falling on ice.

If your dog loves to play in the snow, feed him a little more to make up for the extra calories he burns in winter.

Do not have your dog's fur shorn down to his skin in winter. He needs his winter coat! If your dog is comfortable wearing a sweater, use it.

Wipe down your dog's stomach, legs and paws when he comes in out of ice, snow, sleet or freezing rain.

Prepare a warm bed such as a heavy blanket away from drafts for your pet(s). Mine sleep on my bed and hog the covers but we are cozy and warm and happy.

Some dogs are happiest living outdoors. If that is the case with your pet, or for some reason he must remain outside most of the time, protect him with a draft-free, dry shelter, large enough for him to lie down comfortably yet small enough to hold in his body heat. The dog house should have a floor that is raised two or three inches off the ground and covered with straw or cedar bedding. Cedar bedding is available at farm supply stores and is easier and neater to transport in your car than straw. It also repels fleas and is softer than straw. Towels and sheets are not suitable for outdoor bedding as they get wet and freeze. Position door to the shelter to face away from the wind.

I bought an igloo type dog house for my large dog for under $200. It was easy to assemble and light enough that I could move it around. Since it was plastic, the interior was always dry even through heavy rains. Lad went to Heaven several years ago, but the dog house is still in excellent condition and shelters feral cats to this day.

Feed outdoor pets and strays more in the winter as merely keeping warm depletes energy and burns calories. You might want to mix in canned food along with the dry if you don't already do so. I pour left over gravy and sauce, heated up, over food given to ferals.

Keep water bowls full, and make sure water is not frozen. Use plastic food and water bowls since your pet's tongue can freeze to metal. Remember the iconic Christmas movie with the boy and the flagpole?

Electrically heated water bowls are readily available as are outdoor heated pet beds. As of this writing the beds cost around $55.00.

Microwavable pet bed warmers stay warm for up to twelve hours without using electricity. Heat up in the microwave as needed. These beds cost around $40.

Eddie's joint aches and pains are alleviated – at least to the point he is able to walk – by eating two to four biscuits containing glucosamine, one or two each morning (depending on how cold or rainy it is outside) and one or two in the evening.

Winter Driving Safety Tips.

If you absolutely don't need to go out, stay inside until the weather (and roads) clear.

If your battery is more than three years old, have it checked out before winter sets in.

If you hear a buzzing, grinding or clicking noise when you turn on the ignition, it is time to replace your battery.

Also have your tires checked over before winter and if necessary (or only borderline) replace them. Maintain your vehicle manufacturer's recommended tire pressure. If you don't know how to do this – and I confess that I don't – go to your mechanic, dealership or tire and battery shop and have a professional do it for you.

If your door locks freeze, do not, repeat, do not, pour hot water into the lock. Use a commercial product formulated for this purpose.

Keep your gas tank filled. If you get stranded on the road, having enough gas to be able to keep your car (and heater) running could be a lifesaver. Having your tank filled will also keep your gas line from freezing.

Do not use your emergency brake in cold, wet weather. I found this out the hard way, not realizing that the emergency brake was frozen when my wheels would not move, fearing I had broken an axle. I also don't lock my car in bitterly cold, wet weather for the same reason but this is something only you can decide.

If you do get stuck in snow, stay with your car as it provides shelter. It also makes it easier for rescuers to find you. If you would decide to walk for help, you could easily become as blowing, drifting snow reduces your visibility. You could also get hit by another vehicle.

If your car is stuck in a snow bank, make sure the exhaust pipe isn't clogged with snow ice. A blocked exhaust could cause deadly carbon monoxide gas to leak into the passenger compartment with the engine running.

Keep an emergency kit in your car:
- As always, a fully charged cell phone and car charger. You might want to bring a wall charger as well in case you are rescued and end up at a shelter.
- Flashlight with fresh batteries.
- Bottled water.
- Blankets (my daughter gave me one that plugs into the cigarette lighter).
- Windshield scrape.
- Booster cables.
- Shovel.
- Bag(s) of sand or cat litter.
- Pieces of old rugs or cardboard to help you gain traction if you get stuck.

Driving on snow covered roads.

Drive slowly.

Give yourself plenty of time and room to stop at red lights and stop signs. Slow down enough for the red light to turn green if possible.

Get a little run before getting to a steep hill, then drive with a steady and light foot up the hill. After you reach the top of the hill take your foot off the gas and drive down as slowly as possible. There is a hill at every intersection of the road where I live so I not only allow my car to coast down, but I also put on my emergency flashers. If no one is coming the other way, I gently steer my car onto my road without braking. If there is another car (or cars) heading toward me, I lightly tap my brakes all the way down the hill, stopping as smoothly and safely as I can.

Don't stop on a hill unless it is an emergency (car stalled in front of you, for example). You will lose your inertia, your tires and will spin and get you nowhere and the only solution is to back down the hill and get a fresh start back up.

Thunderstorms.

Indoor Safety.

Do not use a landline during a thunderstorm. Lightning can strike phone lines and electrocute you.

Turn off your computer during storms. Again, you could be electrocuted. Don't use your hairdryer, curling iron, blender or other electrical appliances for the same reason.

Water is an efficient conductor of electricity so don't wash dishes, do your laundry, take a shower or bath or wash your hands during a storm.

Although a thunderstorm puts on quite a show, stay away from windows. It's too dangerous.

Stay inside.

Outdoor Safety.

Darkened skies and increasing winds often are the first signs of an impending thunderstorm. If you hear thunder, immediately go to a safe shelter. Heavy rains often follow.

Your car, with its windows all the way up, is one of the safest places to ride out a storm. If there is a house or barn nearby, seek shelter there.

Stay away from trees as well as metal sheds, fences, clotheslines, bleachers, baseball dugouts and picnic areas.

If you are with a group of people, leave 15 to 20 feet between you.

As previously discussed, water is an excellent conductor of electricity. Stay out of swimming pools and mud puddles during thunderstorms.

Tornadoes.

According to The Federal Emergency Management Agency (FEMA), signs of an impending tornado include dark clouds, large hail, and a loud roar. I can personally attest to the fact that a tornado does indeed sound like a freight train.

In the Midwest, peak tornado season hits in June or July. However, the tornado I survived hit Central Ohio the day after Christmas, 1973. In spring of 1974 (at Easter) it hit again. Although tornadoes can occur any time day or night, most of them hit between 4:00 and 9:00 p.m., with 5:00 and 6:00 p.m. being the deadliest. This means there is a good chance you will be home should a twister head for your neighborhood.

Tornado watch: Possibility of tornadoes in your area. Stay tuned to the radio or television news.

Tornado warning: A tornado has been spotted on the ground or has been detected by Doppler radar. Seek shelter immediately!

You won't have much time to get out of the twister's path, so formulate a plan now. Be prepared. What would you do if a funnel cloud has touched down near you?

The safest place is your basement, but what if you, like many others including myself, don't have one? Since the worst danger comes from broken glass which turns into flying shrapnel, we need to designate a small interior room with no windows, on the lowest level of the house (first floor) as our safe haven. For most of us, this means a bathroom.

A bathtub will provide protection, especially if you cover yourself with pillows; you might also consider keeping a mattress within reach during threatening weather. A bicycle or motorcycle helmet will help prevent head trauma which is the most common tornado related injury.

Mobile homes are particularly vulnerable in a tornado's destructive path. Some mobile home parks have community storm cellars but yours does not, make a plan in advance to take shelter quickly in the event of an emergency.

If you have time to drive to a safe place, make sure that your exit route will be clear. Driving on a road that could be flooded, littered with debris (falling limbs), covered with downed power lines or congested with traffic is too dangerous and potentially deadly. Perhaps you and your neighbors could plan to share a ride. Remember to assist disabled and elderly neighbors if at all possible.

If you plan to use your car to escape, you must do it before the twister hits. Whirlwinds can toss automobiles like they are toy cars.

The National Weather Service recommends that if you are in a car, truck or other vehicle, in a mobile home, or outdoors, and there is no suitable shelter, go to the nearest ditch, lie flat, covering your head with your hands. If you have a bike, motorcycle, football helmet or other protective head gear, use it.

- If you don't have a basement, take cover in a small interior room.
- Get into bathtub and cover yourself with a mattress or blanket to protect yourself from flying glass.
- Wear a helmet. If you don't have one now, buy one for every member of your family and keep for emergency use.
- Don't drive into a tornado.
- If you are outdoors or in a mobile home or car, lie face down in a ditch. Cover your head with your hands or wear protective head gear.

Flooding.

I live in a flood plain area where the road frequently flooded until those in charge took action and had the dam maintained properly.   Although I am fortunate to live on high ground, I learned all about flooding, the hard way.

Never, ever, ever drive through flood waters. Believe me when I say the water is always deeper than it looks and it takes only a few inches for your car to either stall out or get caught in a current.   Losing your car is bad enough, but by driving through flood waters, you could lose your life.

Park your car well out of the way of flood waters. My mother was unable to move hers when a flash flood approached. However, she was safe in her home so things could have been much worse. Be careful when buying a used car, because flood ravaged cars have been dried out, then brought into another state to be sold at auction. These cars can have electrical damage which is expensive to impossible to fix, and the mud will seep through to the interior.

If you have advanced warning, here are a few tips to help you protect your belongs. However, your life is more important that material items, so be prepared to leave, and leave everything behind, if necessary.

If you do not have advanced warning, leave immediately for higher ground. Call 911.

Indoors.

Move valuables and personal treasures above the flood level, upstairs to a second floor if you have one, or on top of your refrigerator, kitchen cabinets and high shelving. Store electrical appliances out of the reach of flood waters as well.

Move sofas, chairs and tables away from walls so that they may dry out after the waters recede. If they are too heavy to move, weigh them down with anything heavy so that they do not float into windows. You don't want to come home to broken glass.

Turn off all utilities and disconnect your washer and dishwasher.

Open all interior and cabinet doors.

Pack a bag of warm clothing including extra shoes and grab any necessary medication in case you need to evacuate.

If you are told to evacuate, do it. Do not attempt to be a hero and stay in your home.

Outdoors.

As earlier mentioned, move your car to high ground, if possible. If you can't, leave it. A car can be replaced.

Unplug outdoor lighting, pool filters, pond pumps and other exterior electrical appliances.

Move lawn furniture to higher ground. This is a low priority so let it go if you don't have time.

If you need help, call 911.

Hot, Hot Weather.

Let's get the scary stuff – heat exhaustion and heat stroke - out of the way before discussing easy ways to get through the hottest weather.

According to the CDC:

Signs of Heat Exhaustion:

- Heavy sweating
- Weakness
- Cold, pale, and clammy skin
- Fast, weak pulse
- Nausea or vomiting
- Fainting

If You Suffer from Heat Exhaustion:

- Move to a cooler location.
- Lie down and loosen your clothing.
- Apply cool, wet cloths to as much of your body as possible.
- Sip water.
- If you have vomited and it continues, seek medical attention immediately.

Signs of Heat Stroke (Heat Stroke is a Medical Emergency):

- High body temperature (above 103°F)*
- Hot, red, dry or moist skin
- Rapid and strong pulse
- Possible unconsciousness

If You Suffer Heat Stroke:

- Call 911 immediately — this is a medical emergency.
- Move the person to a cooler environment.
- Reduce the person's body temperature with cool cloths or even a bath.
- Do NOT give fluids.

Now on to ways to stay cool(er) and enjoy the season which often seems to go by way too quickly.

By taking care, you can enjoy summer.

Wear light colored, summer weight clothing. Your clothes should also be loose fitting. Cotton will keep you cooler than synthetics. Cotton breathes, polyester doesn't.

Unless you are a sun worshipper, avoid being outside between 10 a.m. and 4 p.m. If you must sun bathe, swim, or otherwise enjoy the great outdoors during this time, wear sunscreen. Sunglasses and a big floppy hat will also protect you.

If you don't have air conditioning, and the temperatures are frightfully high (over 90 degrees Fahrenheit), go to the mall (you don't have to spend any money) or spend the afternoon in a movie theatre. Public libraries are also a great place to cool off.

As during any other extreme weather, check on elderly friends and neighbors. If their a/c is out due to a power shortage, ask if they need shelter. If they don't have a/c and are used to living without it, make sure they are able to keep cool.

Window fans are relatively inexpensive ($20 or so). Placing a bowl of cold water or ice cubes in front of a fan will give a bit of a relief from the heat.

Turn off lights, ovens, clothes driers and other heat generating appliances during hot weather. If you have a patio or other outdoor space, fire up the grill. Meat does not claim the exclusive rights to barbecuing. Throw some veggies on the barbee and enjoy!

Corn on the Cob

Mix together ¼ cup butter, 2 ½ Tablespoons grated parmesan cheese and one teaspoon basil or cilantro. Wrap 4 ears of fresh corn (husks and silk removed) in aluminum foil. Grill 20 minutes or until tender. Spread buttery mixture onto corn.

Summer Squash

Mix together 1/3 cup chopped fresh basil leaves, 1 Tablespoon olive oil, 1/8 teaspoon black pepper, 1 Tablespoon grated parmesan cheese and 2 ½ teaspoons lemon juice. Cut 2 or 3 summer squash into ½ inch thick slices, lightly coat both sides with cooking spray. Grill until tender, about 3 minutes. Top squash with basil-parmesan cheese mixture.

Grilled Peach

This one is easy. Thread a cinnamon stick through a ripe, juicy peach. Grill 5 minutes or until tender.

Grilled Potato and Onions

Place two slices potatoes, one half sliced onion, a pinch each of salt and pepper, ½ teaspoon lemon juice and 2 Tablespoons olive oil on a double thickness of a large piece of aluminum foil. Wrap so that contents do not spill out of foil. Grill on the side, covered with a pie plate, for 20 minutes. Sprinkle with fresh basil or cilantro.

Eat smaller meals, more often.

Take showers to cool down. Let your hair air dry. When I was pregnant and living without air conditioning, I took at least three showers a day. Hot water made me feel cooler than cold water.

Sleep in the basement, if you have one.

Place sheets and pillowcases in trash bags, let them chill in freezer for an hour or so before bedtime, then put on your bed.

Freeze water in plastic bottles to help keep you cool. Put them in your bed, in your child's car seat (before you place him in it or while you are out of the car shopping), and carry them with you so you can enjoy ice water.
Keep water filled spray bottles in the fridge so that you can spritz your face and arms.

Store make-up and cologne in your refrigerator. Your lipstick won't melt and your cologne will be refreshing.

Refrigerate witch hazel and spray it on your tired, hot feet.

Sweat without raising your body temperature by eating spicy foods. My go to food is red hot peppers.

If you take medications, check with your doctor to see if they interfere with your ability to tolerate heat. Being out in the sun while taking some prescription drugs will make you dizzy or nauseated.

Never, ever, ever leave children or pets alone in enclosed vehicles. Let's add Grandma to the list.

Don't perform strenuous exercise in the heat of the day. Even going for a stroll at high temperatures puts you at risk for heat stroke or heat exhaustion.

If you must work outdoors, take frequent breaks and stay hydrated.

A swimming pool can be considered a luxury, but a child's molded plastic pool is affordable, easy to clean and takes only a little water. Get a plastic pillow from the dollar store, lie on your back with your legs dangling over the edge, and relax. Afraid you will look foolish? Who cares? It's summertime and the livin' is easy. Indulge yourself with a cool beverage of your choice. You might even get a plastic tumbler with a tropical design and little umbrella from the dollar store.

Mocktails

Cucumber-Mint-Lemon Water

6 cups of water
1 lemon, sliced
1/2 cucumber, sliced
Mint leaves

Mix together and refrigerate overnight. Serve on the rocks.

Cucumber Ice Water

One glass of ice water
One slice of cucumber
Simple!

Lemonade-Iced Tea

Chill equal parts lemonade and iced tea. Another simple recipe!

Ginger-Orange-Pineapple Mocktail

One part orange juice
One part chilled ginger ale
One part pineapple juice

Mix together; refrigerate until chilled; garnish with orange or pineapple slices or mint sprigs.

Orange-Cranberry Soda

One part orange juice
One part cranberry juice
One part chilled club soda.

Mix together, refrigerate until chilled; garnish with mint sprigs.

Mojito (non-alcoholic)

Break mint leaves into small pieces into tall serving glass. Cut one lime into slices, reserving half. One add half of the lime slices and one teaspoon sugar into glass. Squeeze juice from reserved lime slices into glass; add crushed ice. Pour chilled ginger ale into glass until full.   If deserved, use two smaller glasses.

Or, relax the easy way by flipping the top off your favorite beverage – soft drink or beer.

Water Safety.

In the Olden Days people would drive out – or before that, saddle up and ride – to the ol' swimmin' hole. Younger folks still dive into quarries and other dangerous places. Play it safe by going to a beach or municipal pool with lifeguards.

When canoeing or riding in a boat, wear a lifejacket and know your location and destination.

If you don't know how to swim, take a class. The Red Cross offers instruction for people of all ages. They also offer water safety classes.

If you are a swimmer, don't over estimate your ability. Always swim with a buddy.

Don't drink and swim! Alcohol impairs judgment and affects swimming and diving skills.

Carry a cell phone in a waterproof case.

www.ingramcontent.com/pod-product-compliance
Lightning Source LLC
Chambersburg PA
CBHW070944290526
45795CB00003B/1129